Be the Best

SWIMMING

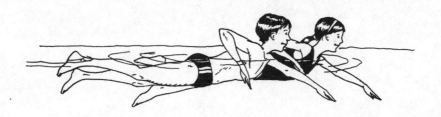

A Step-By-Step Guide

By Gene Dabney

Troll Associates

Library of Congress Cataloging-in-Publication Data

Dabney, Gene.
  Swimming: a step-by-step guide / by Gene Dabney.
    p.   cm.—(Be the best!)
  Summary: Introduces the basics of swimming as well as some
competitive strokes.
    ISBN 0-8167-1945-4 (lib. bdg.)   ISBN 0-8167-1946-2 (pbk.)
    1. Swimming—Juvenile literature. [1. Swimming.] I. Title.
II. Series.
  GV837.6.D33 1990
  797.2'1—dc20   89-27346

Be the Best

SWIMMING

A Step-By-Step Guide

FOREWORD

by Jim Bolster

Swimming is wonderful exercise. It's a great way to unwind, and it's also a terrific sport.

The more you understand the basics of swimming, the better swimmer you'll become. That's why *Swimming, A Step-by-Step Guide,* is such a good source for beginners. It carefully explains those basics, giving you pictures and drills to study and work on. And with practice, the skills you learn here will become second nature to you. Then, who knows? If you keep improving, you may go on to more advanced swimming, perhaps even becoming an Olympic competitor.

But right now, read this book. After that, and with an adult to watch you, hit the water!

Jim Bolster

Jim Bolster has been head coach of men's swimming at New York's Columbia University since 1984. Before coming to Columbia, Jim was head coach of men's swimming at Ohio's Denison University from 1981 to 1984. During that time, he coached the swim team to a #4 NCAA Division Three ranking. As a student, Jim was one of Denison's most successful competitive swimmers, winning All-American honors a total of six times in the 100-yard and 200-yard butterfly.

Contents

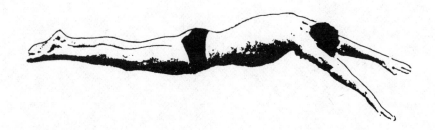

1

The Story of Swimming

More people engage in swimming than any other sport in the world. Almost everyone likes to swim. Of course, not everyone can swim competitively. Competitive swimming takes skill, stamina, and lots of practice. But people of all ages can and do swim for fun, relaxation, and exercise.

Swimming is excellent exercise. It uses all the muscles in the body at once and builds strength in the arms and legs. Good swimmers must use proper breathing techniques, which provide good exercise for the heart and lungs. Doctors recommend swimming as a great all-around exercise for people of all ages.

How did human beings first learn to swim? No one knows for sure. Some evidence suggests that swimming may be a natural instinct of humans.

However, most people believe prehistoric people learned to swim by watching the actions of animals in the water and then imitating those motions. Swimming helped increase the chances of survival for prehistoric people.

The ancient Greeks and Romans were very interested in swimming for fun and conditioning. Julius Caesar, the great Roman general, was a good swimmer. Roman gladiators also used swimming as part of their regular physical training.

Other great swimmers in history included Charlemagne and King Louis XI of France.

However, swimming was not just a pastime for the wealthy. For sailors and adventurers, knowing how to swim often meant life or death if their ship sank. So many of them learned to swim as a precaution.

England introduced swimming as a competitive sport in 1837. The National Swimming Society in England held swimming contests in indoor pools. The only swimming strokes used in England at that time were something like the modern side stroke and breast stroke.

Around 1845, a group of North American Indians traveled to England to swim competitively. English swimmers were shocked when the Indians used an over-hand stroke. They were even more shocked when the Indians won most of the contests because their stroke was faster than the English strokes.

Formal rules for swim meets were first established in 1869 by England's Amateur Swimming Association. In 1878, the first world swimming record was recognized. It was set by E. T. Jones, who swam one hundred yards in sixty-eight and a half seconds. (This is a very slow time compared to modern records for one hundred yards.)

In the late 1800s, English swimmers finally adopted an overhand stroke similar to the one used by the North American Indians years before. The double overhand stroke, as it was called, became popular because of the efforts of an English swimming instructor named J. Arthur Trudgen. Competitive swimming was now on its way to becoming a modern sport.

Frederick Cavill and his family also helped advance the sport of swimming. After emigrating to Australia from England, Cavill observed the swimming style of the local natives. He was greatly impressed by the kicking action of their legs in the water. That kick was combined with the double overhand stroke into what is known today as the famous Australian crawl. In the 1900s, Cavill's family helped spread the Australian crawl to England and the United States.

Eventually the Australian crawl evolved into the American crawl and into the freestyle swimming techniques used today.

Swimming for both competition and fun is more popular now than ever before. This book will teach you the basics of swimming as well as some competitive strokes. So have fun and come on in, the water's fine!

2

Basics of Swimming

To be a good swimmer, you must learn to relax in the water. You must feel comfortable and confident. Do not be afraid of the water.

To get used to the water, learn to swim in a safe location. The shallow end of a pool is best, but a sloping beach with still water is a good spot, too. Until you can actually swim, *always* work with an experienced swimming instructor. Trying to learn to swim on your own is extremely dangerous.

However, there are ways to practice swimming alone without being in the water. For example, some swimming strokes and techniques can be done while lying on a bench or dry land.

OPEN YOUR EYES

Many young swimmers close their eyes while trying to swim. That is not correct. You cannot swim if you cannot see where you are going. The water will not hurt your eyes. It may sting your eyes a little. If it does, do not rub your eyes. Blink them gently to get the water out.

If you get water up your nose by accident, do not get alarmed. Duck your head in the water, wrinkle up your nose, and gently blow the water out through both nostrils together.

BREATHING

To learn to breathe correctly while swimming, stand in water about chest deep. Or do this exercise along the side of a pool. Make sure you have the help of an experienced swimmer.

With your hands on the edge of the pool, open your mouth and take in a short breath through your mouth and nose. Hold it in for a count of five. Then slowly and quietly exhale through your mouth. Do the same thing again. Remember to breathe in and out quietly.

Now try this breathing technique in the water. Draw in a short breath, turning your head to the side as if you are laying your head on your pillow. Close your mouth and put your face in the water between your arms.

After counting to five, exhale through your mouth into the water. Remember to blow out easily. Turn your head to the side and take another short breath. Take your time. Do everything nice and easy.

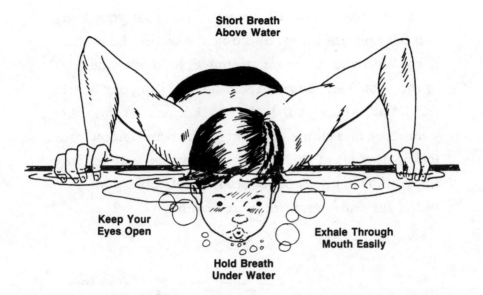

Short Breath
Above Water

Keep Your
Eyes Open

Exhale Through
Mouth Easily

Hold Breath
Under Water

Close your mouth and put your face into the water again. Remember to keep your eyes open. Count to five, then exhale. (Some swimmers also exhale through their noses underwater.) After you finish exhaling, take your face out of the water. Practice this routine several times.

That is how to breathe as you swim. Take short breaths. Hold the air in for a brief count. Exhale into the water through your mouth (and nose, if you prefer). Then lift your face out to inhale again.

FLOATING

Some beginners think that they will quickly sink in the water. That is not true. The human body is naturally capable of floating on the water. Of course, some bodies float more easily than others.

STOMACH FLOAT

The stomach float will prove to you that your body can float on the water. Stand in the water about chest deep. With your arms outstretched, hold onto the edge of the pool. Take a breath and hold it. Dip your face in the water. Allow your body to relax and go limp. Let your chest and stomach lie flat on the water. Allow your feet to rise off of the bottom. The water will actually lift your feet up. After a brief count, take your face out of the water and put your feet down.

STOMACH FLOAT

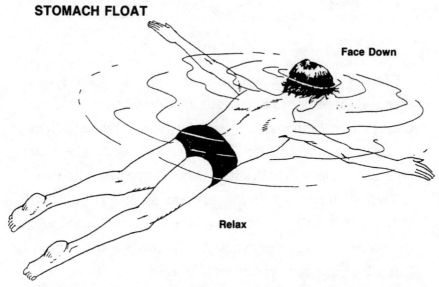

Face Down

Relax

Now try the stomach float without holding on to the pool edge. Stand in chest-deep water. Spread your arms out to the sides. Keep them relaxed. Take a breath, then put your face in the water. Lie in the water on your stomach with your arms out. Allow your feet to rise. Lie calm and relaxed in the water for a few seconds before standing back up.

BACK FLOAT

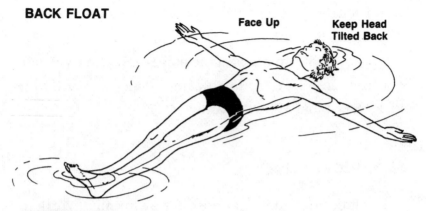

Face Up — Keep Head Tilted Back

BACK FLOAT

Floating allows a tired swimmer to stay on top of the water and rest. The back float allows you to lie relaxed on the water while breathing normally.

Start in water about chest deep. Let your body go limp. Relax. Extend your arms out to the sides a bit higher than shoulder level. Your palms should be toward the sky, and the backs of your hands should be in the water. Lie back on the water with your spine arched just slightly. Your legs should be relaxed but extended, with your feet slightly spread. Keep your face out of the water, your chin up, and your head tilted back.

BACK FLOAT WITH ROWING AND FLUTTER KICK

Arms Gently Row

Don't tense up. Stay calm and relaxed as you float on your back. Breathe easily, taking short, steady breaths.

Easy swanlike motions of the hands and arms will help you remain afloat. You can also do short, easy flutter kicks (see page 19) with your feet.

FACE FLOAT GLIDE

The face float glide is almost like swimming. Work in a shallow area where you can stand up and where there's room in front for you to glide across the water. Take a breath and bend at the waist. Put your face in the water just as you did for the stomach float (see page 14). Keep your eyes open and extend your arms straight out in front, not out to the sides as in the stomach float.

From a crouch position, use your feet to push off from the bottom of the pool. Make it a strong thrust forward. After you thrust forward, lie out on the top of the water. Your body should be stretched out as you glide along the surface of the water. Your legs are straight out behind you. Hold your breath for a few seconds and then exhale into the water.

FACE FLOAT GLIDE

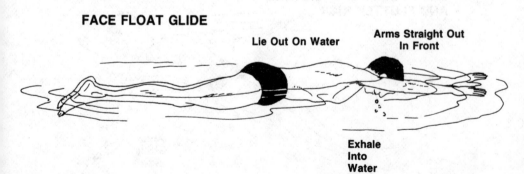

Lie Out On Water

Arms Straight Out
In Front

Exhale
Into
Water

To get back to your feet, draw both knees up to your chest so you are in a tuck position. Then lift your head out of the water, place your feet on the bottom, and stand.

TREADING WATER

To tread water, you must work in slightly deeper water where you may not be able to touch the bottom. As a safety precaution, be sure an experienced instructor is on hand. It is also a good idea to work near the edge of a pool where you can reach out for the edge if you need to.

Assume almost a bicycle-riding position in the water. Your arms should be out to the sides. You should be in a straight-up position with your head out of the water. Move your legs and feet in a bike-riding motion in the water. Draw a knee toward your chest and then gently thrust it straight down in the water. Alternate your legs, going up and down slowly and easily.

TREADING WATER

Arms Forward, Then Back

Hands Cupped

Bike-riding Position Legs Go Up And Down

Place your arms and hands palms down in the water. Cup your hands, keeping the fingers together. Your arms should be out to the sides. Move them slightly forward, then pull them back and slightly down. This motion forces the water trapped in your cupped hands to go downward. It is a sculling or rowinglike motion. It causes the body to bob slightly in the water. Along with the leg kick, it will keep you afloat. You should be very relaxed when you tread water—like you could do it all day if you had to.

3

Elementary Crawl

Long ago, the elementary crawl was called the splash stroke. It was popularized in the 1800s by the famous swimming family of Frederick Cavill. When one of the Cavills described the stroke as "crawling" through the water, the name stuck. It has been called the crawl ever since.

CRAWL KICK

The "kick" is what mainly propels a swimmer through the water. The crawl kick is an up-and-down movement of the feet that's sometimes called a flutter kick.

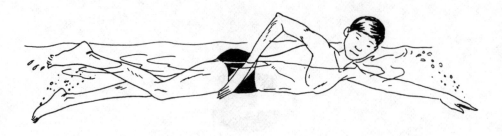

To practice this kick, work at poolside while lying out on the water. Another way to practice is in knee-deep water. Stretch out your arms so your hands rest on the bottom, then lie on top of the water. The kick can also be practiced lying on a long bench on dry land.

To do the crawl kick, bend your knees a little as you kick. Keep your legs stretched almost straight out. The kick action is a loose swinging motion from the hips. Your kick should be slow and easy. It should churn the water rather than make loud splashes. Do not lift your feet out of the water on the upward kick. Your toes should point toward the bottom on the down swing, and they should slightly extend to point behind you on the upswing. Remember, as one foot goes down, the other goes up.

In the crawl, the down kick is more important than the upswing. Do not spread your feet too wide, and do not keep your legs rigid or slap at the water. Relax and kick steadily.

Another way to practice the flutter kick is by combining it with the face float glide (see page 16). An even better way to practice is with a kick board or flutter board, which looks like a small surfboard cut in half. Hold the kick board with your arms stretched out in front away from your body, then flutter kick your way around.

FLUTTER KICK

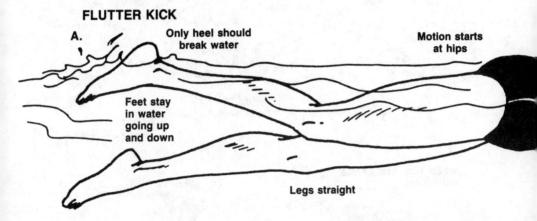

A. Only heel should break water

Motion starts at hips

Feet stay in water going up and down

Legs straight

SWIMMER USING KICK BOARD

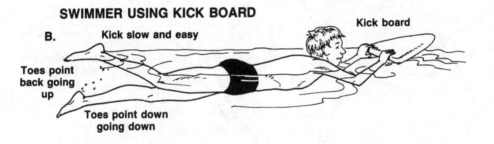

B. Kick slow and easy

Kick board

Toes point back going up

Toes point down going down

CRAWL ARM MOTION

The crawl stroke can safely be practiced lying on a bench on dry land. Another good way to practice is to stand in waist-deep water. Bend forward until your chin touches the water. This way, you can get the feel of the stroke in the water and remain safe.

Remember to cup your hands with your fingers together. That allows you to trap and pull the water. In the crawl stroke, your arms and hands press down and pull the water back to move your body forward.

THE CRAWL'S ARM MOTION

1. Arm Out

Hands Cupped

2. Elbow Comes Out First

Hand Goes Back To Hip

Hand Sinks, Then Pulls Back

3. When Arm Clears Water, Extend Arm

4. Hand Drops Into Water

With your palms down, lift one arm up, bending it at the elbow. Your elbow should rise just behind the ear. After your elbow is clear of the water level, extend it straight out and forward. Let your hand drop into the water with the wrist slightly bent. After the hand sinks about six inches, pull it straight back toward you until it reaches the hip. Now take the arm out of the water again by bending the elbow. Always let the elbow come out of the water first, followed by the hand. The arm has to go up out of the water.

The down, back, and then forward action of the arm is called the arm cycle. In the crawl, as one arm pulls down, the other arm reaches forward. One arm is in the water when the other is out. It is an alternating cycle.

At first, it may be hard to coordinate the motion of the two arms. But after continued practice, you will master it. Remember this important rule: The hand goes into the water first on each arm cycle, and the elbow comes out first.

CRAWL STROKE

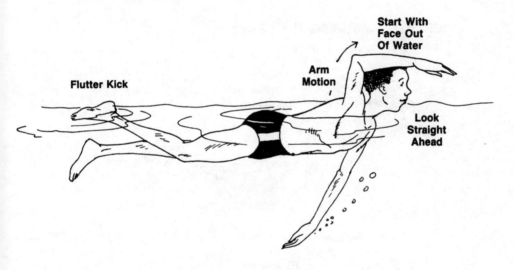

The next thing to do is combine the arm stroke with the flutter kick. First, practice the crawl's arm stroke and kick in very shallow water with an instructor watching you. Do not worry about the breathing process. Just keep your head up and look straight ahead. Only after the kick and stroke are mastered can you learn how to breathe correctly during the crawl.

BREATHING DURING THE CRAWL

To breathe correctly during the crawl, turn your head to the side and up out of the water as you lift your elbow above the surface. Your face should always be turned to the same side for breathing. Select a side that seems most comfortable for you. That side is called the recovery side. As the arm on your breathing side extends forward, turn your face back into the water so you face frontward. Hold your breath for a count and then exhale during the pull-back part of the arm cycle. Repeat this routine.

BREATHING DURING THE CRAWL

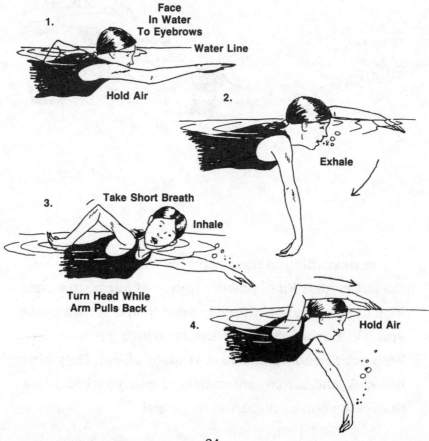

1. Face In Water To Eyebrows
Water Line
Hold Air

2. Exhale

3. Take Short Breath
Inhale
Turn Head While Arm Pulls Back

4. Hold Air

Work on breathing in a shallow part of a pool. Take a breath and put your face in the water (see page 12). Keep your eyes open. Hold your breath and exhale through your mouth. Keep your head down and turn toward your breathing, or recovery, side. When your mouth and nose are above the water line, take a quick, short breath through the mouth and nose. Turn your face down into the water again. Hold your breath for a count, then exhale. Practice this several times.

To work on the arm stroke, kick, and breathing all together requires a helper or some sort of floating tube. The best way is to have a helper hold you up in a shallow part of the pool. Getting all three elements of the crawl to work as one is hard at first. Remember, inhale when the arm on the recovery side is out of the water. Turn your head and raise it high enough so that your mouth is out of the water. Take a short breath. Turn back into the water as the arm goes forward. Hold your breath and then exhale during the downward stroke.

After working with a floating device or a helper for a while, move on to swimming on your own in a shallow part of the pool. If you get tired, just stand up.

When you become a stronger swimmer, try swimming in deeper water. But remember, *never* swim alone!

4

Breast Stroke

Though not as fast as the crawl, the breast stroke is easy to learn and fun to do. It allows a swimmer to go a long way without using a lot of energy. Beginners like it because it can be done without using any difficult breathing techniques.

BREAST-STROKE ARM MOTION

To do the breast stroke, lie flat on your stomach in shallow water. Extend your arms and legs straight out front and back. It is like the glide position used in the face float glide (see page 16).

Sweep your hands out, down, in, and up under your shoulders. Then reach forward for the next stroke.

BREAST-STROKE ARM ACTION

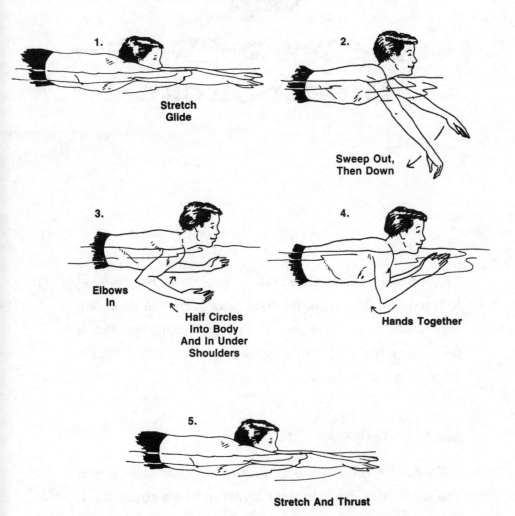

1. Stretch Glide

2. Sweep Out, Then Down

3. Elbows In — Half Circles Into Body And In Under Shoulders

4. Hands Together

5. Stretch And Thrust

Remember to move both arms together in the same manner at once. In the breast stroke, your arms should never come out of the water. Pull your arms and hands downward in a rowinglike motion. Slightly angle your thumbs toward the bottom. Draw your arms toward your chest until your elbows are at about shoulder level.

Now pull your elbows into your body and bring your hands together, thumb to thumb, just in front of your chin. Move your arms in a circular fashion as you draw them back. Then pull them up under your body to join the hands again. Be careful not to let your arms get too far back on the pull stroke. It's a mistake many beginners make.

After joining your hands, thrust them straight out forward again. When the arms thrust forward, the body will glide through the water.

BREAST-STROKE KICK

The breast-stroke kick is nothing like the flutter kick. Sometimes the breast-stroke kick is referred to as a frog kick because of its froglike action. The breast-stroke kick can be practiced while holding on to the side of a pool. It can also be practiced with a flutter board (see page 20).

The breast-stroke kick must work closely with the arm stroke. At the starting position, your arms and legs should both extend straight out from your body (see page 27). As you pull your arms down, bend your knees and draw your heels up toward your rear by lowering your hips and knees. Keep your knees slightly spread as they come up toward the outside of the hip. When your legs are close to your rear, turn your toes out and circle your feet out, down, and in until they come together. Glide through the water. Then hold your legs straight while you start the armstroke again. The kick action should begin as the arms sweep in during the armstroke

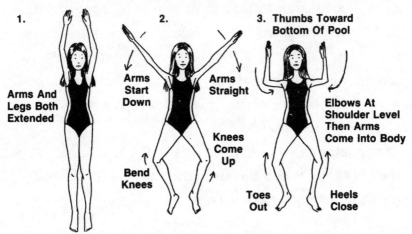

THE BREAST STROKE (Bottom View)

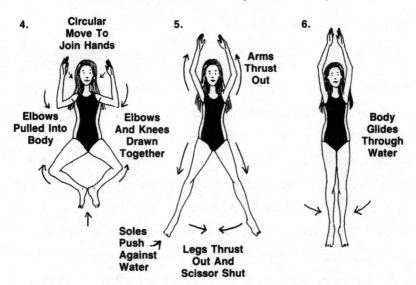

BREATHING DURING THE BREAST STROKE

Some beginners do the breast stroke with their heads out of the water all of the time. Breathing is then quite simple. Just tilt your head back slightly while in the water.

However, there is a proper breathing technique used by advanced swimmers. They lift their heads out of the water to take a breath when they pull their arms back and draw their knees forward. If you advance to this point, make sure your breath is a short one and you inhale through your mouth and nose. Then dip your face back into the water when your hands come together in front of your chin. Exhale during the glide.

BREAST STROKE BREATHING

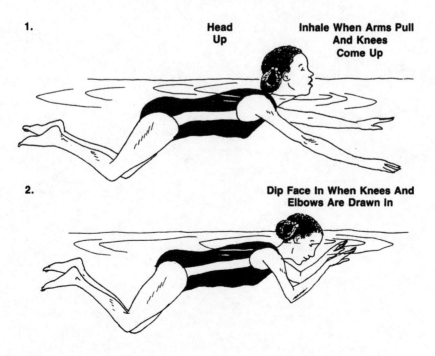

1.
Head Up
Inhale When Arms Pull And Knees Come Up

2.
Dip Face In When Knees And Elbows Are Drawn In

3.   **Hold Breath**

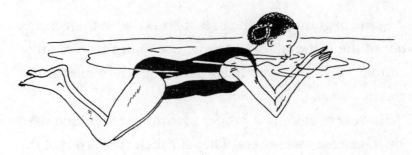

4.   **Exhale During Glide**

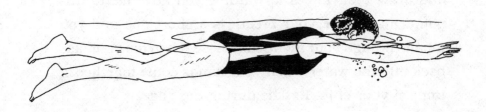

5

Elementary
Backstroke

The elementary backstroke is a very relaxing stroke. It has an easy breathing technique. Because you are on your back, there are no special breathing methods. You can inhale and exhale normally.

The elementary backstroke combines the back float with a breast-stroke kick, which you've already learned (see pages 15 and 29). Those two, plus a sidearm pull stroke, make up the elementary backstroke.

BACKSTROKE ARM MOTION

In the backstroke, both arms do the same thing at the same time. Place your arms at your sides. It is like standing at attention while lying on your back in the water. Be relaxed.

ELEMENTARY BACKSTROKE ARM MOTION

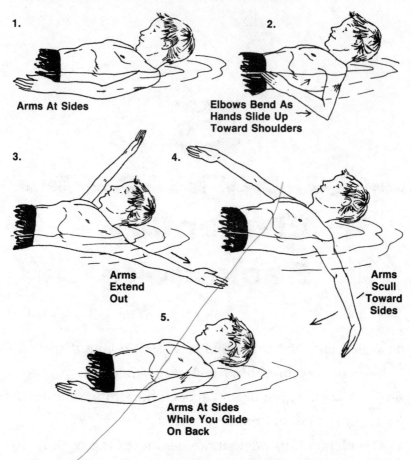

1.

Arms At Sides

2.

Elbows Bend As
Hands Slide Up →
Toward Shoulders

3.

Arms
Extend
Out

4.

Arms
Scull
Toward
Sides

5.

Arms At Sides
While You Glide
On Back

Next, bend your elbows as you slide your hands up the sides toward your shoulders. Your elbows should be held as close to your body as possible.

When your hands reach the shoulders, extend them straight out from your body to the sides. Your hands should be just slightly above shoulder level in the water. The palms of your hands should face back toward your feet.

Next, move your arms back toward the starting position in a sweeping, rowinglike motion. Keep your elbows locked. It is like a flying motion. Your arms then remain at the side in the starting position while you glide on your back.

BACKSTROKE KICK

The elementary backstroke kick is the same kick you learned for the breast stroke (see pages 29-31). The difference is that you'll be swimming on your back, not your belly.

ELEMENTARY BACKSTROKE

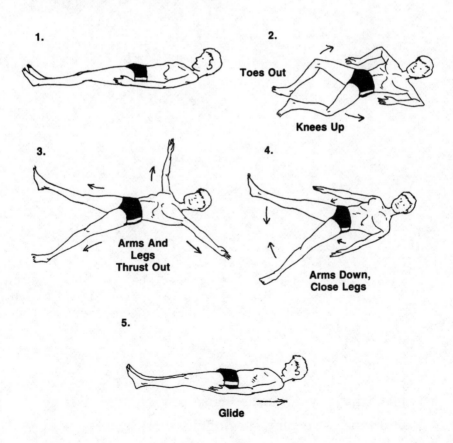

1.

2. Toes Out / Knees Up

3. Arms And Legs Thrust Out

4. Arms Down, Close Legs

5. Glide

To begin the basic backstroke kick, straighten your legs and place your arms at your sides. Now slide your hands up the sides of your body as you draw up your knees. Then shoot out your arms to the sides while thrusting out your legs. It's almost as if your arms and legs separately form a V in the water at the same time. Sweep your arms toward the sides as you scissor your legs close. Hold this starting glide position for as long as possible.

6

Side Stroke

The side stroke is a stroke all swimmers should learn eventually. It is a fun stroke used for distance swimming.

It is also a stroke requiring no special breathing techniques. Because of the body's side position in the water, the mouth and nose are held above water level during the stroke.

In the side stroke, the arm pull and leg kick are difficult to describe separately. The stroke is easier to learn from a description of both motions together.

SIDE-STROKE LEG AND ARM MOTIONS

Remember to practice new strokes in shallow water where you can easily stand. Also remember that if you tire while working in deep water, you can float (see page 14) or tread water (see page 17) to rest.

In the side stroke, start by lying on your side in the water. It's a good idea to learn the side stroke first on one side and then practice it on both sides. Most right-handed swimmers do the side stroke on their left side, as described here.

SIDE STROKE

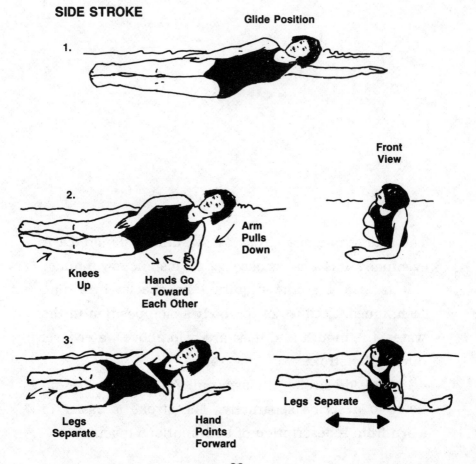

Glide Position

1.

Front View

2.

Arm Pulls Down

Knees Up

Hands Go Toward Each Other

3.

Legs Separate

Hand Points Forward

Legs Separate

Begin by extending your left arm straight ahead. Turn your palm down. Look to the side, not ahead, and hold your mouth and nose above water. The shoulder of your extended arm should be almost against your left cheek. Hold your right arm straight along your right side, keeping your hand near the right hip. Your left hip should be pointed toward the bottom, and your legs should be extended feet together.

To start the stroke, sweep your extended left forearm slightly downward toward your torso, cupping your hand to pull at the water. This arm motion is *not* straight down toward the hip. Instead, it is done at an angle toward the torso and left shoulder. Your hand should end up underwater near the left shoulder and under your chin.

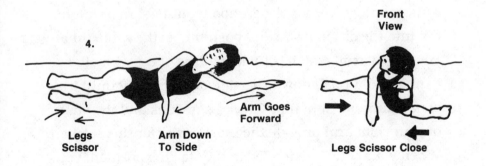

Front View

4.

Arm Goes Forward

Legs Scissor

Arm Down To Side

Legs Scissor Close

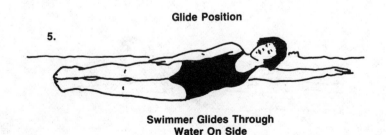

Glide Position

5.

Swimmer Glides Through Water On Side

At the same time, slide your right hand up the front of your body toward your closing left hand. Your right hand should stop when it is about shoulder level. Hold your right hand tucked to your chest.

While your hands are curling toward each other, move both your knees upward, drawing them toward your stomach. Your knees and legs should remain together here, and the heels of your feet should be drawn toward the buttocks. When your knees are just below hip level, separate your legs into a scissors position. Usually the right leg continues to move forward while the left leg moves backward. Remember, you are still on your side.

Your left arm has now finished its stroke. Draw it into your chest and under your left cheek. Your elbow should be bent with your fingers pointed ahead.

As your legs scissor close, shoot your left arm straight out into the original starting position. At the same time, your right arm, which is tucked at the chest with elbow bent, should push down the side of your body until it's alongside your right hip. The scissors kick and the push of your right arm provide the most power for this stroke. When your body is extended in the starting position, you will glide through the water on your side.

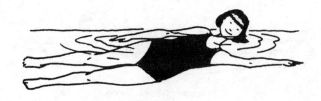

7

Butterfly Stroke

The butterfly stroke was developed in the United States around 1935. It is a quick, double-overarm stroke. The action of the arms looks like the motion of a butterfly's wings, which is how the stroke got its name.

BUTTERFLY ARM MOTION

In the butterfly stroke, both arms work together at the same time. The arms come out of the water in a rotating, circular motion to the sides.

Start with your arms above the water and out to the sides, bending your elbows slightly. Your hands should be bent at the wrists with palms toward your torso.

Bring your arms forward in an overhand motion. Your hands should enter the water with your arms a little further apart than your shoulders. Reach out with your hands. Sweep them in a circle down and out, then in and up until they are nearly together under your chest. Then push the water out, up, and back toward the surface.

BUTTERFLY ARM MOTION

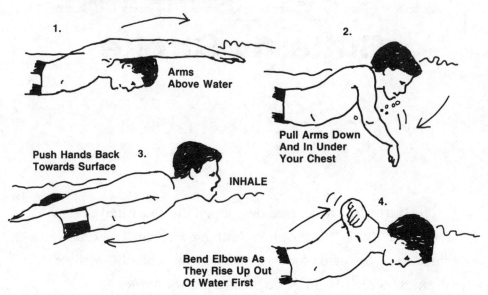

1. Arms Above Water

2. Pull Arms Down And In Under Your Chest

3. Push Hands Back Towards Surface — INHALE

4. Bend Elbows As They Rise Up Out Of Water First

Once in the water, your arms stay extended and start a downward pull straight toward the body. Your hands go in about eight inches deep. Then bend your elbows as you draw your arms in toward the waist. The elbows rise up over the back and out of the water. Remember that the elbows should always come out first, followed by the hands. Your arms should rise completely out of the water behind your ears. The stroke cycle then begins again.

DOLPHIN KICK

The butterfly stroke uses a special kind of kick. It is called a dolphin kick. The dolphin kick is an up-and-down, whip motion of the feet as they are held together with toes extended. It is almost like the movement of a dolphin's tail, which prompted the kick's name.

In the dolphin kick, your knees and legs stay together. The whip action occurs at the waist and knees. Your legs should be bent slightly at the knees. The heels of your feet should be near the surface, with your toes pointed downward. And your back should be arched at the waist, with your seat high in the water (see diagram).

DOLPHIN KICK

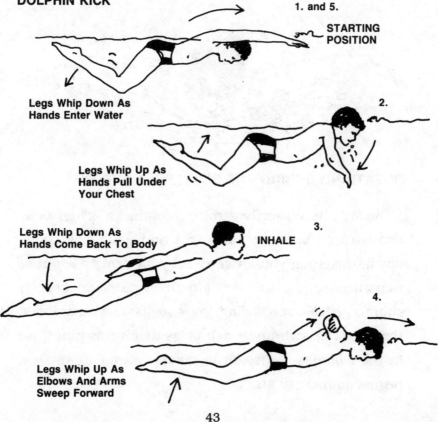

1. and 5.
STARTING POSITION

Legs Whip Down As Hands Enter Water

2.

Legs Whip Up As Hands Pull Under Your Chest

Legs Whip Down As Hands Come Back To Body

INHALE

3.

4.

Legs Whip Up As Elbows And Arms Sweep Forward

43

As your arms come out of the water, extend your back a bit forward. This will decrease the arch of your back. Your legs and seat should sink lower in the water here.

As your arms start their downward pull, straighten your legs. Your seat should rise up as your back and face dip into the water. From a side view, the body is in a slight V position.

As your hands come back toward the body, draw your legs slightly forward, bending them at the knees. Your seat will sink as your back arches up to lift your face out of the water. Try not to let your feet rise out of the water and slap against the surface as you kick.

BUTTERFLY STROKE

BREATHING DURING THE BUTTERFLY STROKE

During the butterfly stroke, breathe in when your hands reach your stomach area and your kick snaps down, thrusting you forward. As your arms rise out of the water, dip your face into the water and keep it submerged as you swing your arms downward and then in. Most swimmers exhale as their arms pull close to their bodies. A breath is taken every two strokes, rather than every stroke.

8

Racing Freestyle Crawl

The key to speed in the racing freestyle crawl is the position of the arms and hands as they enter the water. Your hand should knife into the water straight out from the shoulder. Turn your hand in a little during the pull while the elbow is pointed out.

When your stroke arm is at shoulder level, increase the bend in your elbow. Your hand should continue back to hip level but should not go past the hip. In recovery, raise your elbow out of the water first, followed by the forearm and then the hand.

For purposes of speed, keep your body high and flat in the water. Don't sink too low, and don't arch your back too much or roll your shoulders.

Your arms and legs must work together in close rhythm. Remember to start the leg kick at the hip, not at the knee. For racing, there should be three up kicks and three down kicks for each arm cycle. Your heels can break water, but your feet should remain submerged. The power of your kick comes more from the upswing of your leg than from the downswing.

FREESTYLE CRAWL

BREATHING DURING THE RACING FREESTYLE CRAWL

Inhaling is always done on the same side (your choice of right or left). When turning your head out of the water, go high enough so that you can get a mouthful of air. But do not hold your head out too long. When you turn back into the water, your face should be submerged up to the eyebrows.

In sprint swimming, one breath is good for about twenty-five yards. Two breaths should last for fifty yards. Beyond that distance, take one breath every other stroke.

In long-distance swimming, breathing should be done with every stroke.

Racing Backstroke

The racing backstroke is something like an upside-down crawl. You're on your back, face up in the water. The stroke is an overarm one done backwards that's combined with a flutter kick (see page 19).

RACING BACKSTROKE KICK

To start the racing backstroke, float on your back (see page 15). Instead of holding your legs still, use the flutter kick you learned about in the crawl (see page 19). Keep your legs relaxed. Make sure your toes are pointed. In the racing backstroke, it's mainly the upward motion of your kick that helps propel you forward in the water. The idea is to whip your feet at the ankles without loud splashing.

RACING BACKSTROKE

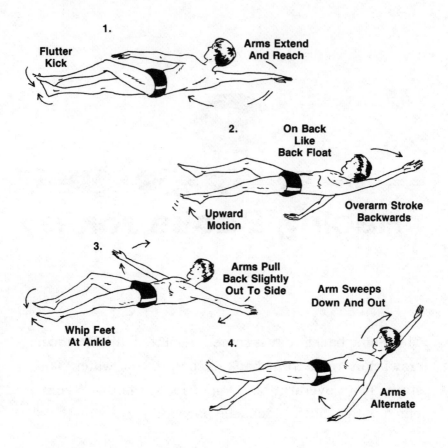

1.
Flutter Kick
Arms Extend And Reach

2.
On Back Like Back Float
Upward Motion
Overarm Stroke Backwards

3.
Arms Pull Back Slightly Out To Side
Whip Feet At Ankle
Arm Sweeps Down And Out

4.
Arms Alternate

RACING BACKSTROKE BODY POSITION

Keep your body flat on the water and your chin tucked to your neck. Your head should be held high enough so you can see the action of your feet.

RACING BACKSTROKE ARM MOTION

Start by placing your left arm along your side and stretching your right arm out behind your head. Keeping your left arm loosely extended, bring it up out of the water. As your arm goes in the air, turn your left palm away from you. Place your hand in the water directly in front of your shoulder. After your hand enters the water, press it down and out. Then sweep your hand in and up toward the surface, gradually bending your arm. When your hand comes near the surface, push the water down toward your feet by extending your arm. Then pull your arm up and straight overhead.

The racing backstroke has alternating arm movements. As your left arm is going over your head toward the water, your right arm is pulling down through the water toward you.

RACING BACKSTROKE ARM MOTION

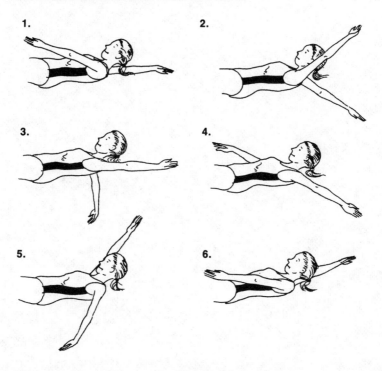

Remember to alternate your arms. One arm should be up and out of the water as the other arm pulls through. Keep the arms opposite. You should be slightly gliding halfway between each stroke.

Breathing during the racing backstroke does not require any special techniques. Just remember to inhale through your mouth and exhale through your nose.

10

Racing Starts

To swim a successful race, you must have a good start. Starting techniques differ according to the strokes used, as described below.

FREESTYLE RACING START

Of all the official swimming competitions held, the freestyle race is probably the most popular. In an official competition, freestyle racers begin from starting blocks. The block is normally thirty inches above the water. The key to a good racing start off the block is a well-timed body spring along with proper technique.

Before taking your mark, relax and breathe deeply. When you hear the command to "take your marks," step to the edge of the starting block. Place your feet so your toes can grip the edge of the block. That will give you a base to push off from. Do not spread your feet too far apart. A bit less than shoulder width is good. Keep your weight evenly balanced.

Stand with your body bent at the waist and your head down. Look down at the water, *not* across the pool. Your knees should be slightly bent. Your arms should hang loosely in front of your legs, with your fingers pointed at the water. That is the ready position.

FREESTYLE RACING START

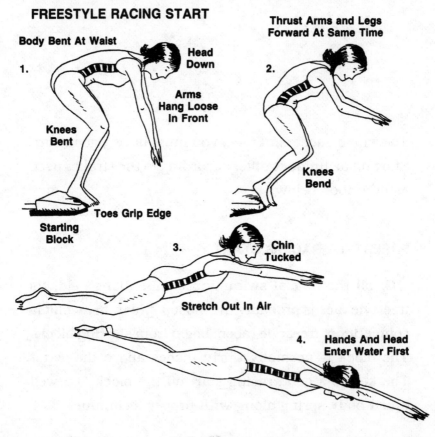

Body Bent At Waist

1.

Head Down

Arms Hang Loose In Front

Knees Bent

Toes Grip Edge

Starting Block

Thrust Arms and Legs Forward At Same Time

2.

Knees Bend

3. Chin Tucked

Stretch Out In Air

4. Hands And Head Enter Water First

On the actual takeoff, swing your arms forward away from your body in half circles. Your knees should bend for added spring. Thrust forward with your arms and legs both at the same time.

In the air, stretch out your body, keeping your chin slightly tucked. Streamline your body in the air. When you hit the water, it should be at a slight angle. Enter hands and head first. Glide underwater briefly, then come up and start to swim.

BREAST-STROKE RACING START

The racing start for the breast stroke is almost identical to the freestyle racing start. There are only a few minor differences, mainly concerning the entry into the water.

RACING START FOR BREAST STROKE

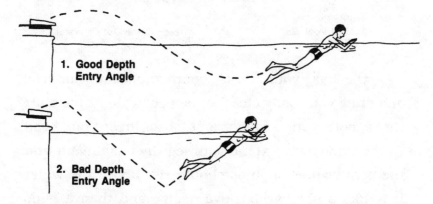

1. Good Depth Entry Angle

2. Bad Depth Entry Angle

For the breast stroke, your entry dive is deeper, and you'll go a distance underwater before coming to the surface. Your dive, however, should not be so deep that the angle of your rise to the surface lengthens the distance you have to swim.

BACKSTROKE RACING START

The racing backstroke begins in the water rather than on a starting block. Line up along the edge of the pool. You'll be looking in the opposite direction from where you'll be swimming.

Now hold on to the gutter rail or the starting holes in the side of the pool. Place your feet side by side against the pool wall, or place one above the other. They can be shoulder width apart.

**STARTING POSITION FOR
RACING BACKSTROKE**

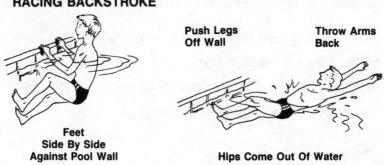

Push Legs
Off Wall

Throw Arms
Back

Feet
Side By Side
Against Pool Wall

Hips Come Out Of Water

On the "take your marks" command, bend your arms and draw your body close to the pool wall. At the start, throw both your arms straight back over your head. At the same time, extend your legs by pushing off from the pool wall. Your hips should rise above the water. It is like a shallow backward dive and then a glide. When the glide slows, begin swimming with the leg kick. Then the arm stroke should follow.

The first arm pull must be done very quickly. This is the pull that will get you into the backstroke position. You can do it with either hand.

11

Racing Turns

Almost all swimming competitions are held in pools rather than open water. Race distances are usually two lengths of the pool—once up, once back. That means you must make a turn in the water at the far end of the pool. There are several ways you can make a racing turn in the pool.

GOING IN FOR SOMERSAULT TURN

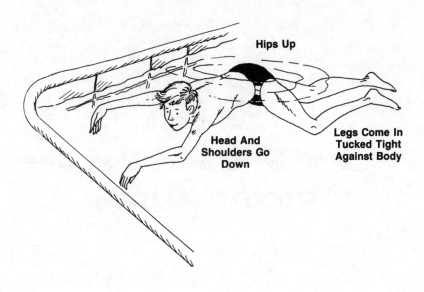

Hips Up

Head And
Shoulders Go
Down

Legs Come In
Tucked Tight
Against Body

SOMERSAULT RACING TURN

The somersault racing turn is the faster of the two turns used in sprint swimming. Your head and shoulders should go down in the water as you tuck your chin toward your chest. Roll into a ball and somersault forward so your legs come over your body and your feet make contact with the wall. Push off the wall, turning onto your stomach as you shoot out.

SPIN RACING TURN

For the spin racing turn, used only when swimming backstroke, the palm of your lead hand should touch the pool wall in front of the opposite shoulder. Turn your head toward the opposite shoulder as you draw your legs into a tuck position.

Keeping your face down, use a sculling motion (push the water away from you) with your free hand to help your body make the spin. After your body turns in a half circle, extend your hands over your head and push off with your legs.

Remember, the spin racing turn is much slower than the somersault racing turn. Most competitive swimmers today use the somersault racing turn.

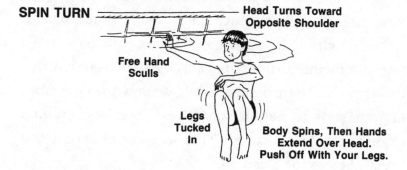

SPIN TURN — Head Turns Toward Opposite Shoulder

Free Hand Sculls

Legs Tucked In

Body Spins, Then Hands Extend Over Head. Push Off With Your Legs.

DISTANCE RACING TURN

The distance racing turn is a slower turn used for intermediate distances. It also helps you get a breath during the turn.

Touch the wall with the palm of your lead hand, keeping the fingers pointed upward. At the same time, roll your body slightly on the side. Draw your legs up under your body as your hand touches. As your body reverses position in the water, swing your feet under your body to come in contact with the wall.

Thrust your lead arm in the direction of the push-off, making sure your head turns with it. Your other arm should also now be extended in the direction of the push-off. Before the push, turn your face slightly toward the wall and take a breath. As you push off, join your hands to cut through the water.

BREAST-STROKE AND BUTTERFLY RACING TURN

During the racing turn for the breast stroke and the butterfly, *both* hands must touch the pool wall at the *same* time for the turn to be legal.

As you approach the wall, extend both arms, keeping your elbows slightly bent. Point your fingers upward. At the touch, tuck your legs up under your body. This is a spin racing turn (see page 57). As your body turns, the arm on the turn side should scull across the front of your body to help it spin. Keep your head up and slightly back as it turns. This way, you can catch a breath before the push-off.

BREAST-STROKE TURN

Two Hands
Touch Wall

BACKSTROKE RACING TURN

A backstroke touch is made with one hand. There are two types of backstroke racing turns: the tumble turn and the spin turn.

In the tumble turn, your lead hand should touch the wall ten to twelve inches under the water. As soon as you touch the wall, your legs should go into a tuck position and your body should go over backward in a somersault. As your feet go over, your body should spin to the opposite side underwater. This way, you'll end up on your back. Keep your head tucked. Otherwise, your spin will go too deep. As your body spins, your free hand helps by sculling.

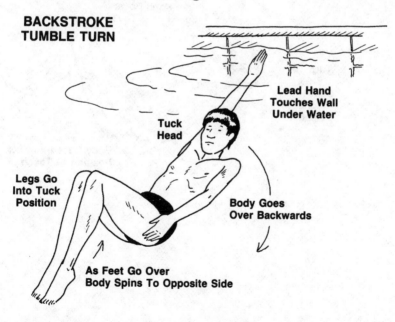

BACKSTROKE TUMBLE TURN

Lead Hand Touches Wall Under Water

Tuck Head

Legs Go Into Tuck Position

Body Goes Over Backwards

As Feet Go Over Body Spins To Opposite Side

With your feet against the wall, push off. Extend both your arms over your head and stretch out your body. Start the arm pull first and then follow with the kick.

The backstroke spin turn is almost like the freestyle spin turn (see page 57). When your lead hand touches the wall, your body goes into a tuck position. Your free hand then reverse sculls to help the turn. It is made to the side opposite the touching hand. As your body spins, both your arms should go back over your head. The push-off from the wall is then made with your legs. Stretch out your body, then start the arm pull followed by the kick.

BACKSTROKE SPIN TURN

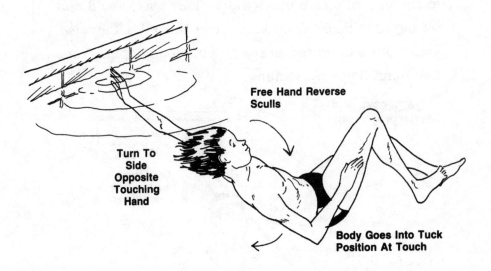

Free Hand Reverse
Sculls

Turn To
Side
Opposite
Touching
Hand

Body Goes Into Tuck
Position At Touch

12

Competitive Swimmers

What physical qualities do you need to be a competitive swimmer? Swimmers come in all shapes and sizes. Swimmers need good strength in their arms, shoulders, and legs. They must also be loose and limber.

CONDITIONING

Building up your swimming endurance takes time. Never keep swimming when you feel tired or weary. Stop and continue the next day.

The more efficient your strokes are in the water, the less tiring they will be to do. So always concentrate on correct technique.

A good swimmer eventually learns how to do all strokes well. Knowing a number of strokes helps in training. For physical conditioning, try to swim a mile in stages. Swim a different stroke in each stage. That way, you won't get bored, and you'll also exercise different sets of muscles. Swimming laps freestyle is another good way to build endurance.

SWIMMING LAPS

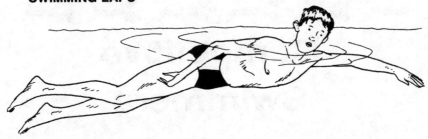

PROPER SLEEP AND DIET

Another important part of competitive swimming is getting adequate rest and nutrition. Eight hours of sleep a night, especially just before a swim meet, is advised. And eat sensibly. Many swimming coaches recommend a light meal three to four hours before a meet. However, *always* wait at least one full hour after a meal before entering the water. If you don't, you may get stomach cramps.

13

Safe Swimming Fun

The water is a fun place to enjoy yourself. But always remember that the water can be a dangerous place. Never swim alone. Also, never swim or dive in a strange place where you don't know what the bottom looks like. Avoid showing off and rough play. If you feel tired or faint, stop swimming and come out of the water. And always obey lifeguards and follow water-safety rules and regulations.

Have a good time swimming. But make sure your water fun is safe fun. Look after yourself. Remember, you're someone important!

INDEX